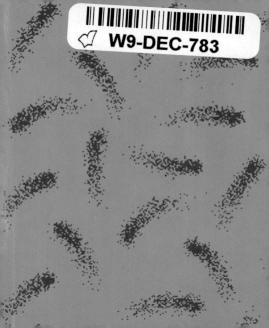

W9-DEC-783

It's About Time 1997!

Coffee

• ARIEL BOOKS •

ANDREWS AND McMEEL • KANSAS CITY

coffee

RANDY BURGESS

C O F F E E

ISBN 0-8362-1053-0

Library of Congress Catalog Card Number 95-80740

CONTENTS

Introduction	7
History	11
The Coffeehouse	21
Coffee-Producing Countries	29
Working the Bean	36
Coffee Quotations	45
The Best Cup Possible	56
Anecdotes and Oddities	62
Coffee in Fiction	74

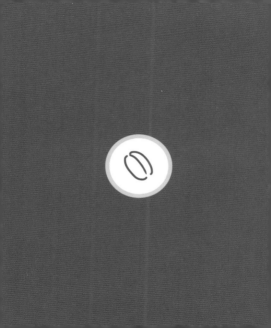

COMFORT and contradiction: Coffee is both, at once familiar and exotic.

What could be more American than a cup of joe? Yet every such cup is a distillation of tropical sun and soil, carried to our shores in the holds of ships steaming from Brazil, Ethiopia, Kenya, Sumatra, Java, Guatemala, Hawaii.

Of all ancient beverages, coffee is the most mercurial. Depending on the alchemy of circumstance, the drinker's mood, and of course the manner of preparation, coffee can be as bright as sunrise or as velvety as evening, as sensible as tea or as romantic as wine. Coffee can inspire, soothe, give you the jitters, prepare you for war or for work. Its taste is as changeable as the rest of its character—smooth or bitter, strong or spicy, dainty or robust, cosmopolitan or country.

A natural anti-depressant, it has been extolled as a medicine and condemned as a poison. Kings have banned it and spies have smuggled it; German hausfraus, English poets, French revolutionaries have drunk it, as have GIs and sailors and private eyes and cowboys and truckers and just about everyone else in America.

Many have praised coffee's genius, its unique combination of energy and pleasure. As Prince Talleyrand, an enthusiast of the previous century, put it: "Suave molecules of Mocha stir up your blood, without causing excessive heat."

On the other hand, a modern writer on the subject, Englishwoman Claudia Roden, has begged to be excused, pleading that her powers of description are not equal to the task. "I cannot find the right words, nor give an identity to the sensations each coffee has given me," Roden tells with wistful passion. "I would far rather put a steaming cup in your hand and say, 'Taste it! Smell it! Look at it!'"

Alas, this book cannot become a cup in your hand, but it can give you a taste just the same—a taste of the sun-dazzled history, of the whys and wherefores of what makes a superior bean and superior brew, and of the collected opinions of coffee-loving philosophers, satirists, and others throughout the ages.

HISTORY

THE CRADLE of coffee is Ethiopia, known in older times as Abyssinia—a land of deserts, highlands, and forested plateaus, perched on Africa's right shoulder and bordering the Red Sea. There, the most prized of the several species of coffee trees, *Coffea arabica*, grew wild for unaccounted centuries before notice was taken by man.

Just how was coffee discovered? We can trace the first written mention of it to the tenth century, in a medical encyclopedia written by Rhazes, an Arabian physician. And experts believe cultivation may have begun long before that, perhaps as early as A.D. 575. But as to who actually made the discovery, there are no facts, only legends.

KALDI

The commonest of these legends is the one about Kaldi, a young Abyssinian goatherd, and his dancing goats.

Kaldi was used to seeing his goats behave in a normal fashion, so when he found the entire herd cavorting and dashing about the field one day, he was astonished. Watching their frolics, he wondered whether it could be something they had eaten. He followed them as they wandered up and down the hillsides searching for food, and soon he observed their partiality to the red berries of a certain short, bushlike tree. Cautiously, Kaldi chewed a handful of the berries himself. He did not have to wait long until, infused by an unexpected wave of energy and delight, he, too, began to dance.

In time, a passing monk, an imam, saw the dancing goatherd and the dancing goats. Kaldi showed the curious holy man the berries and explained their effects. The monk, in turn, introduced the berries to his monastery, where they were pronounced good: they kept monks from dozing and allowed more time for prayer.

THE WINE OF ARABY

Regardless of whether it was Kaldi or someone else who first happened upon coffee's revivifying powers, the practice of chewing the berries, and later of fermenting them to make a kind of wine, spread rapidly throughout North Africa and the Arabian Peninsula. By the thirteenth century, the further refinement of roasting the beans and grinding them had been invented in Persia, and coffee, as we know it today, had finally arrived.

In Arabic, the new drink was called *qahwah*, a word that originally meant invigorating and was also used to describe wine. This same word became the Turkish *kahveh*, which led to the French *café*, Italian *caffé*, Dutch *koffie*, German *Kaffee*, and, of course, our own English *coffee*.

COFFEE

By any name, it was originally regarded as a holy drink, its use restricted to monks preparing for prayer. Later, it was considered a medicine, especially good for curing a cough (today we know that one of the ingredients in coffee and tea is, indeed, effective against asthma). From Mecca, the center of the Islamic holy world, coffee spread to mosques and temples in Cairo, Damascus, Aleppo, Baghdad, all throughout Arabia. Monks began offering it to congregations; by 1475, it had escaped the strictures of religion and was being imbibed in public.

So arose the Kaveh Kanes, the Arabian coffeehouses. They attracted students, artists, travelers, and others, all of whom gathered to sip the drink and escape the heat of the day. Patrons listened to the music of violins and tambourines, or danced, gambled, played chess, sang, argued about religion and politics. As would happen later in Europe, such delightful gathering places inevitably drew the wrath of the powerful: religious leaders frowned on the frivolity, while pashas and beys worried about the subversive effect of all that free-spirited discussion.

Because of this, coffeehouses were occasionally raided and destroyed. In 1656, the Ottoman Grand Vizir Koprili even went so far as to ban coffee entirely; anyone caught drinking the stuff was beaten with wooden cudgels. That was only for first-time offenders; repeat offenders were sewn up inside a leather bag and thrown into the Bosporus.

COFFEE COMES TO EUROPE

When the Ottoman Empire conquered parts of North Africa and Arabia, the Turks took coffee to heart. It became so prized that the failure of a husband to provide a wife with a proper and constant supply of coffee was considered grounds for divorce. In the late 1500s and early 1600s, visitors from Germany and traders from Venice began to take notice.

"The Turks have a drink of black color," wrote Pietro Della Valle of his visit to Constantinople, "which during the summer is very cooling, whereas in the winter it heats and warms the body, remaining always the same beverage and not changing its substance." Historians also point to the Turkish siege of Venice in 1683 as a possible beginning of the passion. In particular, a spy for the Venetians is said to have tasted coffee during his undercover visits among the Turkish besiegers. After the Turks retreated, this confidential agent opened Venice's first coffeehouse, called Zum Roten Kreuz, or At the Red Cross, near St. Stephen's Cathedral.

However it happened, the Venetians smelled a profit. They were already importing Eastern spices, perfumes, silks, woods, and dyes. To this list of exotica was added the coffee bean.

THE
COFFEEHOUSE

IT IS SIMPLE enough to track the progress of coffee through Europe by noting the appearance of coffeehouses.

In 1650, the first coffeehouse opened its doors in Oxford, England, its proprietor a Turkish Jew named Jacob. In France, the first house opened in 1672. By 1843, there were thousands of coffeehouses throughout Europe and the American colonies.

Today's trendy espresso shops bear no resemblance to the coffeehouses of yore.

A true coffeehouse was crowded, smelly, noisy, feisty, smoky, reeking, celebrated, condemned. On the street in London you located the neighborhood coffeehouse by sniffing the air for roasting beans, or by looking for a wooden sign fashioned to resemble a Turkish coffee pot or a sultan's fez. Inside you found everyone from bankers to stock jobbers, shipowners to newspapermen. Samuel Johnson had a coffee club at the Turk's Head; Dryden, Pope, Swift, Addison, and Pepys were all habitués of coffeehouses.

Edward Ward described one London coffeehouse as a sort of cave, with the patrons swarming about like rats in a cheese shop: "Some came, others went; some were scribbling, others were talking;

some were drinking, some smoking and some arguing; the whole place stank of tobacco like the cabin of a barge."

In Parisian coffeehouses, or cafés, as they were called, you found actors and authors—and also revolutionaries. Indeed, were it not for cafés, the French might still be ruled by king and queen. Andrés Uribe Compuzano, in his book *Brown Gold*, paints this picture of the Café de Procope in those gilded, fatal years: "Marat, Robespierre and Danton plotted the destruction of Louis XVI and Marie Antoinette over Procope's tables while Napoleon Bonaparte, a poor artillery officer, devoted himself to playing chess.

It comes as no surprise that such a

popular institution had opponents everywhere. In Italy, priests asked Pope Clement VIII to forbid the infidels' brew; the Pope, finding it delicious, endorsed it. In Prussia, Frederick the Great condemned the increase in coffee consumption as "disgusting" and urged his subjects to drink beer instead.

Women in England, annoyed that their husbands spent so many hours at the coffeehouses rather than at home, circulated a petition in 1674 protesting "the grand inconveniences accruing to their Sex from the excessive use of the drying and enfeebling Liquor." Coffee, the women went on to say, made men as "unfruitful as the deserts where that unhappy berry is said to be bought."

COFFEE IN AMERICA

A couple on the Mayflower brought a mortar for grinding coffee with them to the New World, but whether or not it was actually put to this use is unclear. Only small amounts of coffee beans were imported to the colonies for many years.

Eventually, however, Dutch and French smugglers did introduce beans in great quantity, and coffeehouses opened in New York, Boston, Baltimore, Philadelphia, and elsewhere. Most were more like taverns than genuine coffeehouses, since they served not only coffee but also chocolate, ales, beers, and wines. They also rented rooms to sailors and travelers.

One famous coffeehouse in New England was the Green Dragon in Boston. At first it was popular with British officers, but in later years it came to be the gathering place of John Adams and Paul Revere and other revolutionaries plotting against England.

Despite the increased availability of coffee, however, tea remained the favorite drink of colonists—at least until Britain's King George insisted on taxing its importation so heavily. This taxation, as every schoolchild knows, led to a general boycott of tea and to the Boston Tea Party of 1773, in which 342 chests of tea literally went overboard. Thereafter, tea drinking was frowned upon as a pro-British, anti-

American activity, and coffee became our beverage of choice—a situation that has never changed.

COFFEE-PRODUCING COUNTRIES

COFFEE MAY, indeed, be as familiar to us as apple pie, but no one talks about the coffee tree growing in his backyard, or of making a visit to the coffee orchard outside of town—although here and there a coffee tree may be babied as a show-piece inside an air-conditioned office. Apples are one thing, but the coffee bean is foreign to our soil.

Coffee grows only in the sun-blessed countries that gird the earth's middle. The coffee belt, as it is called, runs roughly between the tropic of Cancer, to the north, and the tropic of Capricorn, to the south; included are the islands of the Caribbean, parts of the Americas, parts of Africa, and all of Arabia, the Malagasy Republic, India, and the East Indian and Pacific islands.

Within these regions, of course, climate varies, and coffee has adapted; but, in general, it is best grown on ground composed of both rich organic matter and disintegrated volcanic rock. This yields a moist soil with good drainage. The tree cannot tolerate frost.

The coffee tree comes in three main species: Robusta, Liberica, and Arabica. The first two, considered inferior in taste and often used for cheap coffees, do well at sea level. Arabica, their aristocratic cousin, prefers high altitudes, sometimes as much as 6,000 feet above sea level. Differences in rainfall, sunshine, and other variables of climate naturally contribute, along with the bean itself and the manner of processing, to differences in savor.

Here are just a few of the coffee countries and what they produce.

BRAZIL. In 1727, a Portuguese captain was so taken with the taste of the coffee served to him during a visit to the governor of French Guinea that he smuggled out some seeds. These he planted at the Portuguese colony of Para, on the Amazon River. Today Brazil supplies nearly a third of the coffee consumed in the world. Of the Brazilian coffees, Bourbon Santos is considered the best for its sweet, mild, straightforward flavor.

COLOMBIA. Some Colombian coffees are sublime. Others are dreadful. Look for Medellíns, which has an acid but pleasant flavor and a strong body, or Excelso, which is nutty and slightly bitter. The best grades are grown in the foothills of the Andes on the thousands of small family farms clustered there.

COSTA RICA. Coffee from the high altitudes of Costa Rica is heavy, acidic, perfumed, and highly regarded. The middle region of the country, the *meseta central*, has soil rich in volcanic ash and dust from three to fifteen feet deep.

ETHIOPIA. Coffee was born here, but be choosy just the same: Longberry Harar, also called Ethiopian Mocha, is excellent, with a mild, vinous taste, but Abyssinian is not nearly as good.

JAMAICA. Jamaican Blue Mountain has been praised as the perfect coffee, but its price is often outrageous; decide for yourself.

HAWAII. Another expensive coffee but probably worth the price is Kona, named after the Kona district of Hawaii. The best of this smooth yet pungent variety is grown on soil located between the volcanoes of Mauna Loa and Mauna Kea.

SUMATRA. If you can imagine a land designed from top to bottom to grow the best coffee in the world, that land would be Sumatra. This westernmost island of Indonesia is hot and rainy, with a densely forested interior and (inevitably) volcanic mountains. With such a beneficent climate and soil, almost any Sumatran coffee is a good bet. Mandheling is smooth and heavy; Ankola, musky; Ayer Bangies, delicate.

TANZANIA. If you can, try to find Tanzania's Kibo Chagga, made by the Chagga tribe on the misty slopes of Mount Kilimanjaro.

VENEZUELA. Excellent coffees are grown on the slopes of the Maritime Andes. Look for Meridas or Caracas, both of which are lightly but distinctively flavored.

WORKING THE BEAN

FOR MOST of us, the rawest coffee we will ever see is the green unroasted bean—pale little half-pebbles filling a jar in some tiny coffee shop. If we are especially enterprising, we may have bought this green coffee and cooked it in a pan or skillet until it turned dark, the way most Americans used to do in the previous century. To appreciate our bean properly, however, we must consider its progenitor, the coffee tree.

To a naive observer this tree would more nearly resemble an evergreen shrub, with broad, glossy, dark green leaves. Properly pruned and cultivated, it stands about six feet tall. It matures in five years, produces as much as two to three pounds of beans annually, although a pound is more typical, and will do so for several decades at least. Prior to fruiting, the tree flowers—a brief, beautiful flowering, according to Claudia Roden, who gives us this description:

"A coffee tree is a rare, magnificent sight when it breaks out into a fragile and delicate white blossom, its fragrance as intoxicating as that of the orange and the jasmine which it resembles. It may bloom alone like a young bride or with the whole farm, a swaying sea of white petals, as beautiful as they are ephemeral."

THE COFFEE BERRY

The berries appear in clusters—first green, then yellow, then deep red. They should be so profoundly red as to appear almost black before they are picked. In Jamaica, farmers know it is time to harvest by listening at night for the sound of finicky fruit-eating bats, which deign to lap only the most succulent berries.

The fruit, which resembles the familiar North American cherry, is sweet and pulpy, but discarded as unimportant.

Underneath the pulp are two flat-faced beans, facing each other. The beans are covered by a tough hull called the parchment; inside that is a delicate inner sheath called the silver skin. Berries with only one round bean are called pea berries; some connoisseurs prefer these to regular beans.

HARVESTING

For the finest coffees, berries must be picked by hand, whether by shaking the tree or by selecting individual berries. Harvesting lasts from dawn to dusk, since the berries, once ripe, are in danger of being cracked and ruined by the sun.

Either of two methods is used for separating the bean from the pulp. In the first, which produces "washed" coffee, the cherries are floated in vast tanks of water, so that the pulp ferments and softens and can be sluiced away. The beans are then dried, either by machine or in the sun, and finally milled to remove the last traces of parchment and silver skin.

With the second method, which produces "dry" or "natural" coffee, the beans are spread out to dry in the sun for several weeks; a hulling machine then strips the dried pulp. This second method is more variable in its results, but does reduce acidity. Many great coffees are produced this way.

Beans are classified and sorted to meet the requirements for different grades. Stones and other foreign objects are removed, as are unripened and discolored beans. Now the beans are packed in heavy burlap sacks, the kind you can sometimes glimpse stacked in the back of a good coffee store. The sacks are stowed in the holds of fast ships, and the beans are on their way, carefully watched to make sure no water drips on them as the ships leave the tropics behind and sail into cooler climates.

ROASTING

The final stage in preparation of the bean is roasting, which is essential in breaking down the bean's woody structure, bringing the oils to the surface, and creating many of the compounds that give coffee its unique flavor. These days, even small coffee shops can afford their own roasters—typically rotating drums through which hot air is passed, combined with a pan into which the beans, once roasted, are dumped for cooling, while an agitator continues to stir them.

The temperature at which beans are roasted may go as high as 450 degrees, but this depends on the character of the beans and the humidity and temperature of the surrounding air. Also crucial is the desired degree of roast—medium for regular coffees and breakfast coffees, dark for a continental or New Orleans flavor, and the very darkest reserved for espresso.

A roasting bean goes through several stages. In the first, in which it is heated to a temperature somewhat below the boiling point of water, the bean swells slightly. Soon the water inside the bean turns to steam and the bean actually cracks as this steam forces its way out.

The next stage comes after most of the water is gone and the polysaccharides in the bean break down into starches, then sugars. The sugars caramelize, darkening the bean.

In the third and final stage, oils in the bean begin to bubble toward the surface; an attentive listener will hear the beans crack yet again inside the machine as these oils emerge. Some dark roasts, such as French roast, continue even after this stage, with the harsh, strong flavor developing fully as the other characteristics are burnt away.

COFFEE &
QUOTATIONS

COFFEE

Coffee:
Black as the devil,
Hot as hell,
Pure as an angel,
Sweet as love.

CHARLES MAURICE
DE TALLEYRAND-PÉRIGORD

I think if I were a woman
I'd wear coffee as a perfume.

JOHN VAN DRUTEN

The morning cup of coffee has an
exhilaration about it which the cheering
influence of the afternoon or evening cup
of tea cannot be expected to reproduce.

OLIVER WENDELL HOLMES

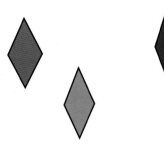

COFFEE

It is disgusting to note the increase in the quantity of coffee used by my subjects and the amount of money that goes out of the country in consequence. Everybody is using coffee. If possible this must be prevented. My people must drink beer. His Majesty was brought up on beer, and so were his officers. Many battles have been fought and won by soldiers nourished on beer; and the King does not believe that coffee-drinking soldiers can be depended upon to endure hardships or to beat his enemies in case of the occurrence of another war.

FREDERICK THE GREAT OF PRUSSIA

If this is coffee, please bring me some tea;
if this is tea, please bring me
some coffee.

ABRAHAM LINCOLN

Coffee: Induces wit. Good only if it
comes through Havre. After a big dinner
party it is taken standing up. Take it
without sugar—very swank: gives the
impression you have lived in the East.

GUSTAVE FLAUBERT

C O F F E E

The coffee was so strong it snarled
as it lurched out of the pot.

BETTY MACDONALD

No coffee can be good in the mouth that
does not first send a sweet offering of
odor to the nostrils.

HENRY WARD BEECHER

After a few months' acquaintance with
European "coffee," one's mind weakens,
and his faith with it, and he begins to
wonder if the rich beverage of home,
with its clotted layer of yellow cream on
top of it, is not a mere dream, after all,
and a thing which never existed.

MARK TWAIN

If you want to improve
your understanding, drink coffee.

SYDNEY SMITH

COFFEE

Actually this seems to be the basic
need of the human heart in nearly
every great crisis—a good hot cup of
coffee.

ALEXANDER KING

Coffee is the common man's gold, and
like gold, it brings to every man the
feeling of luxury and nobility.

ABD-AL-KADIR

There are various theories as to what characteristics, what combination of traits, what qualities in our men won the war. This democratic heritage is highly thought of; the instinctive mechanical know-how of thousands of our young men is frequently cited; the church and Coca-Cola, baseball, and the movies all come in for their share of credit; but, speaking from my own observation of our armed forces, I should say the war was won on coffee.

ILKA CHASE

COFFEE ◆

A cup of coffee—real coffee—
home-browned, home-ground, home-
made, that comes to you dark as a
hazel-eye, but changes to a golden
bronze as you temper it with cream that
never cheated, but was real cream
from its birth, thick, tenderly yellow,
perfectly sweet, neither lumpy nor
frothing on the Java: such a cup of coffee
is a match for twenty blue devils and
will exorcise them all.

HENRY WARD BEECHER

As with art 'tis prepared,
so one should drink it with art.

ARABIC PROVERB

In the interim he takes out of another rag-knot a few aromatic seeds called heyl, an Indian product, but of whose scientific name I regret to be wholly ignorant, or a little saffron, and after slightly pounding these ingredients, throws them into the simmering coffee to improve its flavour, for such an additional spicing is held indispensable in Arabia though often omitted elsewhere in the East. Sugar would be a totally unheard of profanation.

FRANCIS TURNER PALGRAVE

Coffee should be black as Hell, strong as death, and sweet as love.

TURKISH PROVERB

THE BEST
CUP POSSIBLE

THE BEST CUP of coffee, of course, depends not on expensive beans or fancy gadgets, but on circumstance: if it is drunk in the company of friends, or on a morning when your worn soul craves it, or in a romantic inn or restaurant, or when it perfectly suits your mood. Such bliss cannot be bought per pound.

But circumstance aside, there *are* steps you can take if you have your mind, heart, and mouth set on getting that perfect cup of coffee. If you like, you can be extraordinarily fussy; or you can rely on just a handful of essentials, perfectly carried out.

COFFEE

FILTERING VERSUS BOILING. Two basic ways to prepare coffee are filtering—the most popular method—and boiling. Most people who brew their own coffee use paper filters in an automatic drip coffee pot. The idea here is to pour hot water over ground coffee held in a filter, so the grounds stay behind and the drink drips through.

Boiling is how the old-fashioned percolator, often scorned these days, makes coffee; and boiling is, of course, how espresso is made, whether in a fancy machine or in one of those hourglass-shaped pots that sit on a stove burner. The Turks and Arabs make coffee by boiling it, and so did cowboys in the West. In any event coffee made this way tastes stronger, is more bitter and less aromatic, and the body is thicker. Properly done, it is luxury.

WATER. The water you use should itself taste good; for this reason, avoid water laced with chlorine or iron, or any other sort of off taste. The water should also be cold when you draw it, according to experts.

If you are filtering your coffee rather than boiling it, heat the water to just a few degrees below boiling. Any cooler and it can't extract all of the essence from the grounds; any hotter and you will lose some of the aroma and fine taste that filtering preserves.

STRENGTH. The ratio of grounds to water varies with individual preference and the fineness of the grind. In general, with a fine grind, allow from one to two rounded tablespoons of coffee per cup, a cup equaling about seven fluid ounces of water. Your taste should be the judge; if you like it stronger, use more coffee and less water. Be careful, though, when making it weak: don't use less water in preparation but instead dilute the coffee after it is made, to avoid bitterness from overextraction.

FRESHNESS. Green coffee beans can be stored for a long time, but once beans are roasted they lose their freshness quickly. For this reason, try to make sure you buy beans that have been roasted within the last week. Beans that have been sitting in jars forever may look pretty but will have lost their flavor.

As for storing roasted beans at home, whether ground or whole, authorities generally agree that an airtight container is best, but after that they diverge. Some prefer storing in the freezer; others recommend the refrigerator. Both camps will make their arguments. If you use up the beans quickly enough, you won't have to worry about who's right.

POTS. Avoid iron and aluminum when brewing or storing brewed coffee; earthenware and glass are the best choices.

WASHING UP. Clean out your coffee grinder thoroughly, along with the pot, the filter holder, and other equipment. The oil in leftover grounds quickly turns rancid and can spoil the next batch.

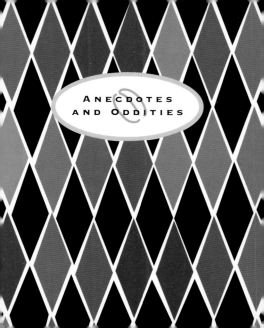

ANECDOTES
AND ODDITIES

The custom of tipping waiters and waitresses began in England's coffee-houses, when patrons began to put money in boxes marked T.I.P., which stood for To Insure Promptness.

The famous international insurance company, Lloyd's of London, originated in a coffeehouse—in fact would never have existed but for the conviviality and commonality of interests the coffeehouse brought together.

Edward Lloyd started his coffeehouse on Tower Street, before moving it in 1692 to Lombard Street. Merchants, bankers, and seafarers favored Lloyd's as an informal spot to meet and do business; so too did underwriters, who insured ships for the payment of a premium. Eventually the underwriters formed an association and named it after the coffeehouse.

Coffee was often taken as medicine. At one time or another it was prescribed as a guardian against the plague; a remedy for gout; a cure for scurvy; a tonic for barren women who longed to be fertile; and a tonic for fathers who longed just as deeply to be sterile, so that their large and expensive families would grow no

larger. Green coffee was sold by apothe-
caries and used by doctors, midwives, and
chemists throughout the seventeenth century.

A verse of that period described coffee's powers with such enthusiasm that
many words had to be rendered com-
pletely in capitals:

Do but this Rare ARABIAN Cordial Use,
And Thou may'st all the Doctors Slops
    Refuse.
Hush then, dull QUACKS, your
    Mountebanking cease,
COFFEE'S a speedier Cure for Each
    Disease.

For Union soldiers during the Civil War, ten pounds out of a hundred-pound ration of food was coffee. Soldiers would mix their coffee and sugar rations with water and boil it over a campfire. In addition to being a pleasing drink, coffee also served to rid their biscuits of bugs. Labels on boxes of hardtack, a kind of biscuit, recommended breaking up the crackers into a strong, hot cup of coffee so that one could fish the weevils out when they swam for shore.

Americans used to make coffee in some pretty funny ways, or so we would think today. In the 1880s it was common to stir in eggs and boil them along with the grounds. Then, when milk or cream was added, it gave the coffee a yellowish color. Lacking eggs, you were advised to add a few squares of dried codfish skin.

Out in the Wild West, coffee had to simmer for hours on end before being pronounced drinkable. It was even better if it had simmered not just for hours but for days. Whatever dinged-up old pot it was made in was never washed, so as to keep all the accumulated flavor and aroma of a thousand makings. The goal was a coffee strong enough to get up on its own hind legs and walk, as the cowboys put it.

In the days of the clipper ships, when San Francisco's Barbary Coast was notoriously dangerous, the owner of a particular café became popular for his habit of serving free coffee at the end of the evening. Since coffee had reached the expensive price of five dollars a pound, customers were glad to take advantage of his generosity.

Eventually, however, a sharp-eyed patron realized that men who indulged in the evenings were missing the following mornings. When his own brother disappeared, this customer, wielding a barrel stave as a persuader, confronted the café owner and forced him to reveal the truth: he'd been spiking the free coffee with a knockout drug, so as to provide short-handed ships with sailors.

In Arabic lands, a coffee-drinking ritual has persisted for centuries when greeting and honoring visitors. It begins with gestures, greetings, praise to Allah, and other formalities. Rules of etiquette govern everything that is spoken and done; coffee is served in small cups the size of half an eggshell.

Refusing a host's coffee is a dire insult; equally insulting is not serving coffee to a visitor. The coffee itself is brewed in a long-handled metal pot called a *kanaka* or *ibrik*; in some cases the coffee is freshly roasted and pounded in honor of the visitor.

Once brewed, the coffee is poured into each cup with a quivering hand, the quivering ensuring that every cup has a nice touch of foam. Bedouin nomads serve cups half filled; a full cup would mean that the visitor is to drink up and get out.

Coffee served at a wedding or birthday is sweetened; at a funeral it must be drunk black.

When Frederick the Great banned the consumption of coffee in Prussia, he employed coffee smellers, who stalked the streets sniffing for the outlaw aroma of home roasting.

The English adventurer and orientalist Sir Richard Burton reported that ambergris, the waxy substance cast off by sperm whales and once used in perfumes, was also commonly added to coffee in the Middle East. Another English orientalist, William Lane, mentions that ambergris was added to coffee in his account of nineteenth-century Egypt. It was a custom of the wealthy, in particular, and it resulted in a delicious fragrance.

During Prohibition, Americans ended up drinking as much coffee as they once had drunk beer. By 1932, coffee imports had risen 250 million pounds a year. Even after Prohibition was repealed, coffee consumption continued to rise.

Coffee has a history of having been smuggled, and, in fact, we wouldn't be drinking it today were it not for a series of enterprising thieves.

Early in the seventeenth century, a devout Muslim smuggled seeds out of Mecca back to his native India, where he planted them in the town of Mysore; to this day Mysore is known for its fine coffee. Later, Dutch sailors stole coffee shoots from India's Malabar Coast and planted them in the Dutch colony of Indonesia. Gabriel Mathieu Desclieux, a French captain of infantry, smuggled a coffee tree out of King Louis XIV's royal hothouse in Paris, then carried it onboard ship in a glass-topped chest all the way to Martinique, where he planted it. It flourished and led to many coffee farms, and eventually descendants of this same plant were carried to Jamaica, Haiti, Guadeloupe, Puerto Rico, Cuba, and the Latin American mainland.

COFFEE
IN FICTION

When he draws out the coffee from the machine, it's thick and black like crude oil. . . . In the tall glasses the drink is dark as an old oak tree and has an overwhelming, almost perfumed tropical scent.
—Peter Höeg, *Smilla's Sense of Snow*

Mrs. Weddington was involved with her coffee. She inhaled the warm fragrance for a long time, took a tiny sip, then set the cup back on its saucer and pushed it deliberately to the far side of the table.

"Oh, I do miss my coffee," she sighed.
—James Crumly, "Dancing Bear"

A real art student wears coloured socks, has a fringe and a beard, wears dirty jeans and an equally dirty seaman's pullover, carries a sketch-book, is despised by the rest of society, and loafs in a coffee bar.

—John Bratby, *Breakdown*

He could not remember which way he made coffee. He could remember an argument about it with Hopkins, but not which side he had taken. He decided to bring it to a boil. He remembered now that was Hopkins's way. . . .

The coffee boiled as he watched. The lid came up and coffee and grounds ran down the side of the pot. Nick took it off the grill. It was a triumph for Hopkins. He put sugar in the empty apricot cup and poured some of the coffee out to cool. It was too hot to pour and he used his hat to hold the handle of the coffee pot. He would not let it steep in the pot at all. Not the first cup. It should be straight Hopkins all the way. Hop deserved that. He was a very serious coffee drinker.

—Ernest Hemingway
  "Big Two-Hearted River"

A whistling sound, like a locomotive's, and a cloud of steam rise from the coffee machine that the old counterman puts under pressure, as if he were sending up a signal . . . while the customers at the counter raise their little cups and blow on the surface of the coffee, lips and eyes half shut. . . .

—Italo Calvino
If on a Winter's Night a Traveler

In an effort to get the coffee going, Bolivar had spilled a small pile of coffee grounds into the grease where the eggs and bacon were frying . . . [This] enraged Augustus, who liked to achieve an orderly breakfast at least once a week.

"I guess it won't hurt the coffee none to taste like eggs," he said testily. "Most of the time your eggs taste like coffee."

—Larry McMurtry, *Lonesome Dove*

After a heated argument on some trivial matter Nancy . . . shouted, "If I were your wife I would put poison in your coffee!" Whereupon Winston [Churchill] with equal heat and sincerity answered, "And if I were your husband I would drink it."

—Consuelo Vanderbilt Balsan
Glitter and Gold

The text of this book is set
in Bauer Bodoni, and the display in
Copperplate Gothic 33 B/C.

Book design, illustrations,
and typesetting by
JUDITH STAGNITTO ABBATE

The staff wishes to thank coffee
for making this book possible.

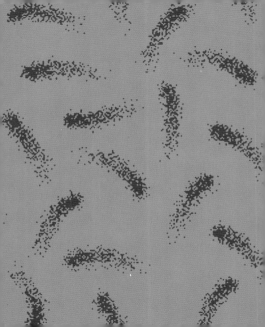